The ORIGINAL
GLORY
of MAN

The ORIGINAL
GLORY
of MAN

JUSTIN ABRAHAM

XULON PRESS

Xulon Press
2301 Lucien Way #415
Maitland, FL 32751
407.339.4217
www.xulonpress.com

Paperback ISBN-13: 978-1-66281-606-2
Ebook ISBN-13: 978-1-66281-607-9

TABLE OF CONTENTS

ACKNOWLEDGEMENTS

"JUSTIN ABRAHAM HAS EMERGED IN THIS HOUR to capture the heart and love of Jesus Christ. Justin is a lover of Jesus and a thoughtful Berean of the word of God. I could not put down the book as it is full of rich treasures and foundational truths. I was captivated by Justin's revelation and simplicity and enjoyed his message with scriptural references. Your understanding of God's love, plan and purpose will be revealed to you, and your faith will soar like never before. Be prepared to receive a fresh passion to see God's Kingdom manifest in your life and courageously taking the gospel of Jesus to your world with confidence. I am so blessed to personally know Justin and can testify his walk is pure in heart and a new wineskin for our generation. Every seeker, Christian and ministry leader should read this book."

Terry Hilgen,
Founder and Senior Pastor, Reign Christian
Fellowship Church, San Juan Capistrano, California

To my friend and brother in the faith, who carries the heart of God in all that you do. Your faith in God has brought you through many seasons in the valley, that's why you have a deep reverence for the mountaintop encounter that you steward so well. Your desire to know Jesus is like a burning wildfire that spreads when anybody encounters you. Your humility and love for people is inspiring which is definitely a true mark of a disciple of Jesus that fervently burns for him. So grateful to call you family, love you brother.

Pastor Marvin Waitman
Refuge House

PROLOGUE

FOR SEVERAL YEARS, GOD HAS BEEN PUTTING it in my heart to truly understand the meaning of identity and how it plays such a significant role in our lives. Growing up, I was a very naïve child and always minding my own business with a very imaginative mind. Along with all of that, I grew up in a very conservative, close-knit, Christian family. Every single night for as long as I can remember, my family and I would sit down to read a chapter in the scriptures every night. We would just read each verse but go through it in depth as much as possible. Afterward, we would sing a few songs in English and Malayalam, our native tongue. At the end of it, we would each say a prayer before going to sleep. Growing up in my house was fun and enjoyable in my childish mind with a fantastic relationship with my parents and younger brother.

This was my norm, and despite my upbringing and growing up, I started to explore the world of music and media through my peers' influence. As I kept digging in, my roots kept me from really going all in. I got more and more into the emo scene, at least mentally, and the hip hop and R&B on the outside. Mentally, I became a wreck. Outwardly, I just wanted to please everyone and even got baptized with my brother and church friends so that people would not think of me as a heathen. I was struggling in sin, depression, and I was a wreck. I always kept to myself because it was frowned upon, and my church community could not fathom how a good Christian boy could be battling depression and sin.

I had slowly been losing the grasp of my identity. I did not know who I was anymore, and I started to have this anger and hatred towards my amazing and loving parents. With my peers' influence and what I heard from those around me gave me a disdain for my parents and upbringing. I constantly started fighting with them because I somehow had this idea that they, especially my father, were bad people. That they never treated me right or loved me the way they ought to.

As soon as I started community college, I started hanging out with a group of friends that I allowed to influence me. This was when the roots of my upbringing started to loosen their grasp on me. I began to get involved with things I should not be dabbling with. Soon, to escape from that, I dove in deeper to get my mind from this torture of being depressed. During this time, a few of my friends that were on this same route I was going in were murdered. Coming out of my friend's memorial service, I picked up a quarter on the floor, and the back of it said, "*Live free or die*." A reality check set in. I started to ponder what the heck I was doing with my life, wasting it away in this mess. That was the prodigal son moment, remembering where I came from and all the prophetic words spoken over my life from pastors and leaders I never knew.

I remember talking to my friend Mitch and asking him, "What the heck are we doing with our lives? I'm tired of playing these stupid charades of life and don't want to live on my parents' couch until I'm 40 years old. February 10, 2010, I made the most significant decision of my life. I gave up the lifestyle I was living and wanted to live all out for God. I made the choice of going on what everyone calls a Daniel Fast. I remember having a conversation with God, and He reminded me that Daniel did not choose to fast for 21 days. He fasted until he received the breakthrough that he was looking for. He also was fasting in a way that was normal in Israel of that time, which was not to eat or drink until the sun went down.

I told God, "I don't care how long I must fast. I will do it for as long as it takes," as I was just so hungry for Him. As a result, my fasting ended up being 32 days. In that time, I had some of the most radical encounters that launched me on the course I am in today. I began to go on this journey of understanding my identity in Him. The adopted son of a King and the bride to the Prince of Glory.

By understanding who I am and where I belong, there was a rekindling of the relationship between my parents and me. Today, the relationship between us is not entirely perfect, but we are in such a better place compared to all those past years. I am writing this book for those who are still struggling with their identity. I want to take you on a journey for you to know who you are, why you are, where you belong, and who you belong to. I pray that the blessing of God is showered upon you daily. Furthermore, I pray that you may experience a deeper level of intimacy with our Lord and Savior Jesus, who has given His all so that you are redeemed by Him.

Through my Christian life experience, I realized that one of the ways to increase my faith in Christ is by understanding the systematic theology of Christ. As we all want our faith in Jesus to progress, our understanding of systematic theology needs to increase as well. Christianity is so badly divided in the Christian world, and it is difficult for a new believer to grow in the Holy faith arising from God's deep love. To understand the love of God and a way of rejoicing in His legitimacy through this beautiful art of exalting Him with our enlightened eyes of discernment. With this understanding, it is essential to see how theology relates to God and his revelation, weighing the sources of theology and why it is necessary for our daily lives.

As you go through your journey in knowing who God is, you will come to realize that all his commandments come under two specific sections. Jesus spoke of them in Luke 10:27 tells us to love our God with our whole heart as the first commandment and our neighbor as ourselves as the second greatest commandment. All others follow suit after. Romans 5 reveals that nothing in any world can separate us from God's love for us. 1 John 4:8 tells us that His most significant attribute of who He is, is *LOVE*. God has also created us in His exact image and likeness (Genesis 1:26). Going through this journey of knowing God helps unlock our identity in Him, and that will cause our spiritual, academic, and churchly discipline to grow better daily. Because of scientific theories in our school system today, it is essential to hold fast to our faith in God so that we are not influenced by contradictory facts that the world throws at us. As we gain the knowledge of our Creator's identity, we will gain the courage through the Holy Spirit in disciplining every area of our lives.

Being faithful in our walk with God is vital in our theology and relationship with God. "And all these, having obtained a good testimony through faith, did not receive the promise, God having provided something better for us, that they should not be made perfect apart from us" (Hebrews 11:39-40 NKJV).

INTRODUCTION

KNOWING THAT WHAT WE BELIEVE TRULY dates back several millennia ago to the beginning of creation. The scriptures challenge us to accept and live according to the cost of knowing Jesus and his ultimate truth. I believe that the scriptures and the Church's tradition of theology go hand in hand because the Church cannot function without the use of the Word. The theology of the Church is unearthed from what it states in scripture, as our way of life depends on it.

The scriptures are used to authenticate the Church we have today and the fundamental doctrine we believe in. The scriptures are God-inspired and given to man through the revelation in Him so that we can have a much deeper and personal relationship with Him. As a minister of the scripture, we need to understand our theology to be more fruitful as we plant seeds and water those we are called to minister to. Titus 1:10-16 tells us that there are false prophets and such and need to be put away from the Church and stopped, and to do this, we would need to understand the systematic theology of the Christian beliefs to us by God through the scriptures.

Understanding our belief system and where it all came from is very important in our spiritual walk with our God above because it brings out some questions for us to get to know.

Why were we created when God knew we would fall into such a sinful nature? Why did God allow man to fall into sin? Who created all of this? Who is God?

Many of us ponder on these questions from time to time. It changed the course of humanity, and we tend to look at it as the beginning of history. The truth is that it is the effect of which was caused by the sin of man. To understand who our Creator is, humanity's creation and fall, the building up to man's eternal redemption, and our purpose are the building blocks to live life to the fullest of our abilities. This means that there's more to the beginning of mankind. There is more to man than meets the eye. And I want to take you on a journey into the past, where everything began.

WHO IS THE TRINITY?

Before we dive into the creation of humankind, we must first understand where we came from and who created us. It is important to understand the Trinity. To know that God is three persons in one.

Before we dive into the creation of humankind, we must first understand where we came from and who created us. It is essential to understand the Trinity. To know that God is three persons in one.

Our faith depicts a Triune God that consists of the Father, Son, and Holy Spirit. The different persons of the Godhead each perform a significant role in executing the divine plan to bring salvation to the world. God the Father sends the Son into the world, while the Son ministers the Holy Spirit's power to the Church. In contrast, the Spirit brings glory to the Father and Son.

1

The Third Godhead of the Trinity is seen in action firsthand in Genesis before the creation of the earth. The Old Covenant reveals that the Spirit of God coming down now and then to bring His message to the prophets. The new covenant shows that the Father perpetually begot the Son with the help of Holy Spirit. 'And the angel answered and said to her, "The Holy Spirit will come upon you, and the power of the Highest will overshadow you; therefore, also, that Holy One who is to be born will be called the Son of God" (Luke 1:35 NKJV). This is disclosed in an intimate approach used to recognize the Father, Son, and Holy Spirit in who they are as the Trinity. The Bible exposes the Holy Spirit's authority through Jesus Christ coming back from the dead and ascending to Heaven and the Church being formed on the Day of Pentecost. Our understanding of the Trinity is given through the Nicene Creed. The Council of Nicaea created this creed in 325 A. D. to better understand our Creator through the lens of the scriptures.

"I believe in one God,
the Father almighty,
maker of heaven and earth,
of all things visible and invisible.
I believe in one Lord Jesus Christ,
the Only Begotten Son of God,
born of the Father before all ages.
God from God, Light from Light,
true God from true God,
begotten, not made, consubstantial with the Father;
through Him, all things were made.
For us men and for our salvation
he came down from heaven,
and by the Holy Spirit was incarnate of the Virgin Mary,
and became man.
For our sake he was crucified under Pontius Pilate,
he suffered death and was buried,
and rose again on the third day
in accordance with the Scriptures.
He ascended into heaven
and is seated at the right hand of the Father.
He will come again in glory

3

to judge the living and the dead

and his kingdom will have no end.

I believe in the Holy Spirit, the Lord, the giver of life,

who proceeds from the Father [and the Son],

who with the Father and the Son is adored and glorified,

who has spoken through the prophets.

I believe in one, holy, catholic and apostolic Church.

I confess one Baptism for the forgiveness of sins

and I look forward to the resurrection of the dead

and the life of the world to come. Amen."

FATHER

"One God and Father of all, who is over all and through all and in all." (Ephesians 4:6 ESV).

"When I consider Your heavens, the work of Your fingers, the moon and the stars, which You have ordained" (Psalm 8:3)

The Father is the first person of the Trinitarian God-head. Jesus makes more than 150 different references to God the Father. Throughout the Old Testament passages, we see the Father's work in the lives of the Israelites. In the book of Matthew, the author reveals God the Father to be the covenant, God of Israel, while Jesus is identified as both the seed of Abraham and David.

John 14:9 says, "Jesus said to him, "Have I been with you so long, and yet you have not known Me, Philip? He who has seen Me has seen the Father; so how can you say, 'Show us the Father'?"

"Yet for us there is one God, the Father, from whom are all things and for whom we exist, and one Lord, Jesus Christ, through whom are all things and through whom we exist." (1 Corinthians 8:6).

"Blessed be the God and Father of our Lord Jesus Christ, who has blessed us in Christ with every spiritual blessing in the heavenly places" (Ephesians 1:3).

"One God and Father of all, who is over all and through all and in all." (Ephesians 4:6).

God, the Father, loved the world so much that He chose to send His only Son to rescue all creation from being eternally separated from Him. Our humane understanding of father figures stems from understanding who the Father is and His love for us. In my relationship with the Father, He gave me a sense of what His love encompasses, which can only scratch the surface with our limited ability of understanding.

In the Hebraic culture, there are two ways of saying Father. Some years ago, God had given me a dream. In this dream, I was holding this beautiful baby girl in my arms, and I just knew that was my daughter. At that moment, all this love just started to pour out of me onto her. I kept telling her, "No matter how many times I have to change your diapers, no matter how many times you upset me, no matter how many times there are disagreements, I will never stop loving you. I will use every ounce of my strength to provide for you and protect you. I will love you to my very last breath. I will use all the resources I have for you. I will give you everything I have." In that moment, the dream freezes, and the roles get switched. Suddenly, God is the Father, and I become that baby. Then He tells me, I love you like that, but exceedingly and abundantly even more than that."

One of my favorite songs that genuinely resembles the heart of the Father is the song *"How Deep the Father's Love for Us"* by Selah:

How deep the Father's love for us
How vast beyond all measure
That He should give His only Son
To make a wretch His treasure
How great the pain of searing loss
The Father turns His face away
As wounds which mar the Chosen One
Bring many sons to glory.

This is just the surface of understanding the Father's love for us. At the moment of humanity's fall, the Father formulated a plan of redemption to bring us back to Him through the sacrificing of His Son. It is indeed through the Father's love that Holy Spirit moves His creation to receive Jesus into their lives as the sacrifice that was offered in their place so that they may be with

Him for all eternity. "The Spirit you received does not make you slaves, so that you live in fear again; rather, the Spirit you received brought about your adoption to sonship. And by Him we cry, "Abba, Father."" (Romans 8:15).

JESUS CHRIST

The early Christians called Jesus is called the "eternally begotten" with a legitimate reason, which may be hard for unbelievers to comprehend. Jesus is the third person of the Godhead whom we refer to as the Son of God. In John 3:16, the Father himself declared, this is my only Begotten Son" and that word in the Greek text is used about sons and daughters.

"In the beginning was the Word, and the Word was with God, and the Word was God" (John 1:1 NKJV).

This passage tells us that Jesus is also referred to as the Word of God. "And they heard the sound of the Lord God walking in the garden in the cool of the day, and Adam and his wife hid themselves from the presence of the Lord God among the trees of the garden. (Genesis 3:8 NKJV). The transliteration for "the sound" is voice.

According to John 1:1, "In the beginning was the Word, and the Word was with God, and the Word was God."

The Greek word for Word is logos, which transliterates to a word that is uttered by a living voice. According to John, the Word is Jesus Christ. In Genesis 3:8, when it states that the sound of the Lord God walking, it is talking about Jesus Christ walking in the garden in the cool of the day. The Hebrew word for presence is *'paniym,'* which transliterates to "face." So, when it says the presence of God, it is saying that Adam and Eve hid from being able to see God's face. This passage strengthens the claim even more of John 1:1 of the Word representing Jesus Christ.

Jesus is the core of all Christianity. Without knowing Him or what He has done for us, we would not be here today. He is the Word who became flesh, to be sin for us.

"For God so loved the world, that he gave his only Son, that whoever believes in him should not perish but have eternal life" (John 3:16 ESV).

The establishment of the covenant was done through the death and resurrection of Jesus on the cross of Calvary with the promise of eternal life for those who believe in him as Lord.

My favorite daily devotional in Max Lucado's book called ***Grace for the Moment***, says:

"The final prayer of Jesus was about you. His final pain was for you. His final passion was for you. Before He went to the cross, Jesus went to the garden. And when He spoke with His Father, you were in His prayers... And God couldn't turn His back on you. He couldn't because he saw you, and one look at you was all it took to convince Him. Right there in the middle of a world which isn't fair. He saw

you cast into a river of life you didn't request. He saw you betrayed by those you love. He saw you with a body that gets sick and a heart which grows weak… On the eve of the cross, Jesus made His decision. He would rather go to Hell for you than go to heaven without you."

It is only through Jesus' sacrifice that He made for us that we are even able to have an eternity to look forward to. Through Him, we see the ultimate version of the love a bridegroom has for His betrothed. "Husbands, love your wives, just as Christ loved the church and gave himself up for her, to make her holy, cleansing her by the washing with water through the word" (Ephesians 5:25-26). A love so sacrificial, that He was willing to sacrifice Himself so that He may present, His bride (the Church), holy and blameless, before the Father (v. 27-33).

HOLY SPIRIT

"It is the Spirit who gives life; the flesh profits nothing. The words that I speak to you are spirit, and *they* are life." (John 6:63 NKJV)

"And the Lord God formed man of the dust of the ground, and breathed into his nostrils the *breath of life*; and man became a living being." (Genesis 2:7 NKJV)

In the "breath of life", the word breath, is נְשָׁמָה, which transliterates to spirit. This shows how the Holy

Spirit is the giver of life and how the Triune Godhead is etched into humanity's very being.

Because the Father, Son, and Holy Spirit are three-in-one, also known as the Trinity, they work in sync with one another. With the Father's pledge and the authority of Holy Spirit, Jesus was born into the world as a man. Isaiah 11:2 says that Holy Spirit will rest on the One to come and brings wisdom and counsel through the fear of the Lord. Romans 8:11 uncovers that through the power of Holy Spirit, Christ was raised back to life. In Acts 1, it confirms that Jesus was brought back to glory through the power of the third Godhead of the Trinity. It is Holy Spirit in Himself who brings conviction to us as we read the scriptures.

As the influence of the Spirit fell on the followers of Jesus on the Day of Pentecost, the Church was birthed, and its numbers were amplified exponentially. On that day, more than three thousand people were added to the Church because of the outpouring of His power in the upper room. Through Holy Spirit, we have become part of one body through baptism despite the cultural background we come from.

"by stretching out Your hand to heal, and that signs and wonders may be done through the name of Your holy Servant Jesus" (Acts 4:30 NKJV).

This passage tells the Church to carry out Holy Spirit's work with the power given to us in the name of the Son. As we are called to bring the Gospel, the Holy Spirit does his work to move in those around us to bring them back to glory. We are to plant seeds and water, while it is the power of God that moves in the hearts of man to salvation.

The Trinity is the abstract of the whole of the Christian faith in salvation and reveals the work of each person of the Godhead working together to bring redemption to humanity (Bird, 2013). Holy Spirit is the One who brings revelation of the love of the Father and the Son for us to comprehend his redeeming work in and through us. Through the guarantee of the Father, the Holy Spirit's supremacy is revealed through Jesus Christ's resurrection and ascension into Heaven, as well as the birth of the Church on the day of Pentecost.

THE CREATION OF HUMANITY & THE ENTRANCE OF SIN

"In the beginning…"

WHEN GOD CREATED THE EARTH, HE SPOKE it into existence. Then there was the creation of everything, living and nonliving. Soon after came the origin of man.

"Then God said, Let Us make man in *Our **image***, according to *Our **likeness***; let them have dominion over the fish of the sea, over the birds of the air, and over the cattle, over all the earth and over every creeping thing that creeps on the earth. So, God created man in His own image; in the image of God He created him; male and female He created them." (Genesis 1:26-27 NKJV)

"And the Lord God formed man of the dust of the ground, and breathed into his nostrils the breath of life; and man became a living being." (Genesis 2:7 NKJV). When humanity was first created, we were created in such an intricate way by the Trinity.

Sin entered the world because of the interaction between the serpent as he persuades Eve to eat the forbidden fruit, which Adam eats. Adam and Eve lost their original innocence, where they were suddenly aware of their nakedness. They also lost immediate access to God's presence. Then Cain murders his brother Abel out of jealousy because God had favored Abel's sacrifice over his. From that point on, mankind became so sinful and rebellious that God was forgotten among them.

Because of the rampant sin in the world, the flood occurred. Despite the flood, the generations after Noah built the Tower of Babel because humanity thought they could get closer to God with it, and their pride was seen, which God did not like. To prevent it from being completed, God gave every one of them a different language.

If God is an all-knowing and powerful God, why did He allow sin and death to enter the world? Which if He was, He would not have let it happen, or so we believe. But we see through the scriptures that because of God's nature, He created humanity to have free will. Although to look at sin and such, we would have to go deeper into history to the time when it was just God and the angels. We know that they are considered messengers and mighty powerful celestial beings, but they also have a free will of their own. Otherwise, Lucifer and one-third of the angels would not have fallen away. The entrance of sin came from the fall of one-third angels.

"Then the serpent said to the woman, "You will not surely die. For God knows that in the day you eat of it your eyes will be opened, and you will be like God, knowing good and evil" (Genesis 3:4-5 NKJV).

Because of Lucifer's hatred toward Almighty God, he entered the dwelling place of God's creation and influenced mankind to let sin into the world, although in the most subtle way possible. Through man's disobedience, sin entered humanity consequently for the human condition. Yet, it's deprivation of the good and how God used it to show His redemptive attribute to deal with this issue.

The scriptures reveal that the focus of humanity went from looking to God to look to themselves. The pride of humanity caused the fall because they were convinced by the serpent that they would be like God by making Eve question the very command God gave them (Genesis 3:4-5). It became part of the human condition to focus more on self than looking to God.

It is clearly seen throughout several places in the Old Testament, such as building the Tower of Babel because they wanted to reach God in Heaven (Genesis 11:1-9). In literature and almost any form of media, we see the human condition in its entirety, whether it is the issue of pride, lust, greed, murder, or the corruption of the heart.

Yet, in the New Testament, despite the corrupted heart of man, God fulfilled his promise of a way of redeeming humanity, which was foretold from the very moment of man's fall (Genesis 3:15). Just as the law was given through Moses to the Israelites, Jesus fulfilled the law through his death on the cross.

As the commandments come under the umbrella of loving God first. As a person gets into a relationship with God, their love for God increases because of their revelation of God's love for them. In that, the person can love themselves more because they start to see themselves the way God sees them, and in turn, are able to love those around them because of the overflowing love and understanding of their Creator.

In that same way, Jesus says that the second greatest commandment is to love your neighbor as yourself (Mark 12:30-31). Because of His relationship with the Father and overwhelming love for his neighbor, He chose to fulfill the law in its fullness by being the sacrifice for their redemption (John 3:16).

"Therefore, just as through one man sin entered the world, and death through sin, and thus death spread to all men, because all sinned" (Romans 5:12 NKJV).

God gave all His creation the ability to make their own choices in life. In doing so, He allowed them to pick between good and evil and in which there would be a consequence behind each thought or action. Without good, there cannot be evil. Without light, there cannot be darkness. The biblical idea of sin is any action or thought that goes against the love of God. Because of sin entering through Adam, all creation was affected because mankind was given the task to rule over the earthly domain (Genesis 1:28). The consequence of man's sin caused the rest of creation to decay, which in turn caused sickness and death as the dominion was transferred to the principalities and powers of darkness.

After their disobedience, God declared how mankind would be punished, that women would bear unimaginable labor pains when giving birth, and that men would be toiling and laboring to make ends meet and such. Although death is not really mentioned until Noah's time when God states that the length of man's age would be reduced to 120 years, we see that it only takes effect several generations later as even Abraham lived way past the ripe old age of 120 years. God relates to us in several different ways, which is how we were created to be like him (Genesis 1:26), through relationship for all eternity, and by intimately loving us despite our shortcomings.

God responds to the sin of humanity, first through correction and then redemption. Understanding what sin is, is a vital part of Christian theology because it is for this reason that Jesus came to redeem humanity from being ruled by sin and death. With Jesus taking the keys of Hell and using His body as a living sacrifice, He made way for us to allow Himself into our hearts and reconnect what was lost between God and humanity during the fall.

"And I will put enmity between you and the woman, and between your seed and her Seed; He shall bruise your head, and you shall bruise His heel" (Genesis 3:15 NKJV).

God quickly set the plan in motion for humanity's redemption. God could have chosen to ultimately cast out Adam and Eve and condemn them for all eternity as he did with Satan and one-third of the angels, but because of how man was created, in the exact image and likeness of God. Man was created for a purpose, which was to reflect God's glory (2 Corinthians 3:18). He reveals His most significant *attribute* to humankind through His redemptive act, which is love (1 John 4:8).

Throughout the Old Testament, the Jewish people have forsaken God on multiple occasions, and because of that, there were consequences. Yet, God still came through and forgave and restored them every single time, even though at times it took longer than others. Being the God of love, the Creator of Heaven reveals Himself to man through Jesus Christ and instructs how to be like Him because that was what humanity was created for. Jesus, Himself, states, "Are we not all (g)ods?" (John 10:34).

He shows us through 1 Corinthians 13 that every act, especially what is done in His name, must be through the love of God and nothing else. Without the love of God, nothing will have profited from it.

God's nature is to give his creation the freedom to choose between right or wrong, love or hate. Newton's third law states that for every action, there is an equal and opposite reaction. In the same way, whatever thought or action that is made causes an inevitable outcome to occur, whether positive or negative.

"And just as you want men to do to you, you also do to them likewise." (Luke 6:31 NKJV).

This free choice was given to all creation, including the angels that can be seen in Ezekiel 28, which revealed Satan's actions before he fell like lightning from heaven (Luke 10:18). Because of man's disobedience, sin subsequently embedded itself into human nature, yet its essential need of the good, and how God used it to reveal His actual characteristics through redeeming creation from this matter. Yet, even during man's sin, Holy Spirit steers man's hearts as the buoys that mark the channels in the oceans to guide them toward wiser habits that help make themselves and those around them better than before. The moment man sinned, man was punished, but at the same time, man's restoration was set in motion.

WHY WERE
WE CREATED?

God is a consuming fire.

ANYTHING IN HIS PATH THAT IS NOT OF HIM
will get burned up. When coming before the throne,
even the angels cover their faces because looking at the
face of God is too overwhelming. Yet, man has been
privileged to be created in His image and likeness;
through purification entering the throne room to see
our Creator face to face. Our God is a relational being.
He made us for fellowship. He walked the earth
alongside man.

But after the fall, how is it that Moses could see the
face of God? Well, at first, he couldn't because God
Himself said that Moses would be destroyed if he did.
As time went by and Moses spent more time in His

presence, God's glory purified him. Moses was refined by His power. Moses' relationship with his Creator was so well-founded that he was finally able to see His face.

When comparing the rest of creation to the way man was formed, God spent a little more time on us. But why? Why did God take time to create us? What was so important that we had to be made this way? Who were we created to be?

God created humanity to be relational, loving, self-less, kind, joyful, does not envy, does not keep any records of wrongs, does not delight in evil, not easily angered (1 Corinthians 13:4-7). We were created in the image and likeness of God (Genesis1:26). 1 John 4:8 tells us that God is love in all its entirety.

"Then God blessed them, and said to them, 'Be fruitful and multiply; fill the earth and subdue it; have dominion over the fish of the sea, over the birds of the air, and over every living thing that moves on the earth.'" (NKJV)

In Genesis 1:28, when God created humanity, He gave us the task to subdue the earth. In the Hebrew text and Strong's H4390, the word fill is מָלֵא (maw-lay), which means to ordain and consecrate the earth. The dictionary definition of ordain is to invest with sacerdotal (priestly) functions. Because God is a holy consuming fire (Hebrews 12:29), anything that comes near Him gets consumed, and we see that first hand in Exodus 33:21-23. He called us to consecrate the earth so that we may have a constant interpersonal relationship with Him. This is still our mission even after sin entered the world because of Jesus' decree to be a blessing to those around us and bring the good news of the redeemer who came to save us all from sin and death.

He created us to have dominion over the earth and to have fellowship with Him. He created us because He needed something to embrace His love to, especially because God IS love. Through our dominion, man was given the task to fill the earth. Consecrate means to make or declare sacred; set apart or dedicate to the service of a deity. God is a Holy celestial being.

Genesis 1 mentions in-depth the creation of man. Man was made in the exact image and likeness of God. The word "image" in the Hebrew text is translated to the word "idol" because that is the only time that word is used in the Hebrew text in reference to that word. This is not to show that we are gods, rather the level of authority and power that was placed on us from the moment of creation. We were created to have rulership of this realm of Earth. The word "likeness" in Hebrew translates to "counterpart," and the definition of that is precisely like and has the same function as the other person.

In being made in the image and likeness of God, the commandment, Jesus gives us so that we can be and act more like him because 1 John 4:8 tells us that his most prominent characteristic of who He is, IS love. Not that He has love, but that He IS love. Even when looking at the ten commandments that God gave the Israelites at Mt. Sinai and all the laws of Leviticus, they all fall under three umbrellas, but at the same time have a trickle-down effect from the first umbrella.

The first few commandments are about keeping God first and having a relationship with him. When we have a relationship with Him, we start to comprehend His love for us, and we go on a journey to love God the way He loves us and loving ourselves as well. As we learn to love ourselves, we can love those around us because of God's love for us overflowing onto them. He created us to be exactly like Him. He created us to pour His love out on us and, in turn, to do the same to everything and everyone around us.

Because God IS love, when we love on others-
When we bless those who curse us.
When we love our neighbors as ourselves.
When we love our enemies.

We are opening the doors of their lives so that God Himself can invade their lives and they can have that God encounter that their spirit-mand has been waiting for, whether to be refreshed or resurrected.

But for us to be able to walk in love with others. We need first to KNOW who love is.

But, how can we know this love?

The only way is through our relationship and friendship with our Almighty Creator. As we choose to draw near to Him, He will draw near to us (James 4:8).

God is Agape.

"Agape is the most selfless form of love there is possible. It does not lose heart. It is virtuous. It is not envious or is not in contentious rivalry with another. It does not boast oneself even to exaggeration. It does not act in the flesh. It is not indecent. It does not require or demand something that is not theirs. It is not made angry or irritated. It doesn't think any evil. It does not deal fraudulently or deceitfully with others. It rejoices in love and speaks the truth always. It has confidence in all things. It has a confident expectation of the eternal salvation of all. It bares bravely and calmly of all things. Agape will never perish because it is eternal." (I Corinthians 13:4-7 NKJV)

"The image of God indicates that you also have remnants of his character within you, and may include the capability

to love – even those who seem unlovable, the capability to create for purpose or simply for beauty, the ability to reason on a very high level, the ability to explore the universe, the capability to communicate with our Creator and to consciously worship Him, the ability to sacrifice for others, a sense of justice – able to be fair, and a built-in sense of right and wrong – morality. This is true for all people, regardless of one's worldview or religion or whether one believes in God or not. But Christians have been called to an even higher purpose – to be conformed to the image of Christ (Rom. 8:29), that is, restored to the perfect image of God; a process sometimes called sanctification that takes a lifetime. The body of a Christian is referred to in 1 Corinthians 6:19-20 as the temple of the Holy Spirit, and as such, you are to purify yourself, being transformed by the renewing of your mind (Rom. 12:2)."

*(-Dr. **Luke Hoselton.** Christian Worldview Professor at Grand Canyon University)*

The Holy Spirit was sent to us so that he could restore and consecrate those who have been justified through their faith in Jesus Christ. The evidence of this is seen through the fruits bore from the gifts of the Spirit. Whoever has faith in Christ and accepted Him into their life as Savior and Lord have become set apart from the powers that control the world.

"Whose minds the god of this age has blinded, who do not believe, lest the light of the gospel of the glory of Christ, who is the image of God, should shine on them" (2 Corinthians 4:4 NKJV).

Living a life of good intentions will not be enough to enter the kingdom of God. It is only through Holy Spirit that we are saved, and through Him, we can do what He has called us to do with the love He has showered on us. The difference between living a contemporary life and spiritual life is that it can easily bear false fruits. In contrast, spiritual practices help mature the Christian faith because of the Spirit's atoning work through salvation and support the launch and perfecting of the kingdom of Heaven.

The contemporary age is based on the nature of humanity according to the culture of the current age, which also means that the moral and ethical values change as different societies rise and fall. Man is selfish by nature because of the entrance of sin and death into this world.

"For the flesh sets its desire against the Spirit, and the Spirit against the flesh; for these are in opposition to one another, so that you may not do the things that you please." (Galatians 5:17 NKJV).

This way of life is a means without the Holy Spirit's work in your life.

Often, when good actions toward relationships and certain practices are produced, they are done out of the heart's selfish desire. Because God judges the purposes of our hearts, He can see when our decisions we make control the way we see things as they become uncompromising and challenging. A contemporary lifestyle being that it is without Holy Spirit's work coming alongside shows that it is worthless in the end. Because God is love (1 John 4:8) and a holy consuming fire (Hebrews 12:29), when it is time to stand before His throne room at the end of our earthly life, everything we have ever done will be set on fire, and we will receive our reward in heaven according to what remains (1 Corinthians 3:13-15).

According to 1 Corinthians 13, no matter what we do to benefit those around us, if we don't do it out of the love of God, it will not profit us a thing. Without Holy Spirit's guidance, we cannot begin to comprehend the love of God and therefore cannot act on it or benefit us in the end.

As a follower of Jesus Christ, there are many things that one undertakes to strengthen their faith and grow into a deeper relationship with him.

"Put to death therefore what is earthly in you: sexual immorality, impurity, passion, evil desire, and covetousness, which is idolatry... But now you must put them all away: anger, wrath, malice, slander, and obscene talk from your mouth (Colossians 3:5,8 ESV).

To live a spiritual life, one must not conform to the ways of this world, which is controlled by the principalities and powers of darkness. Follow the moral and ethical values that are led by Holy Spirit and bring every thought captive to the obedience of Christ (2 Corinthians 10:5). Whoever governs your heart regulates the way that you act. Through a lifestyle of prayer and walking in love with one another through his love (Matthew 22:39), we can walk out the lifestyle of a spirit-filled believer.

Holy Spirit uses Christ's requiting work to us through our salvation so that we can take part in His work in launching and completing His kingdom by bringing it here. It is only through Holy Spirit himself who draws all men to know Christ on a personal level.

"For Christ also died for sins once for all, the just for the unjust, so that He might bring us to God, having been put to death in the flesh, but made alive in the spirit" (1 Peter 3:18 NASB).

It is the Holy Spirit who brings us our spiritual life to reestablish and reconstruct us by washing away and renovate our hearts so that we could have a deeper and more personal relationship with God. The third Godhead of the Trinity works in us so that good fruit may constantly be produced through us, which are love, joy, peace, patience, kindness, gentleness, longsuffering, faithfulness, goodness, and self-control (Galatians 5:22-23). Through this spiritual life, we can reconnect with

God and for his works to be revealed and glorified throughout the earth through his body, the Church.

The Spirit of God was ultimately sent by the Father, just as Jesus had promised. This is so that He could guide us into all truth, and Jesus claimed that it was better for us if He came than for Jesus to stay with them. The gifts of the Spirit are the evidence given to us by God as proof of His promise of eternal life in Him. Living a spiritual life is necessary to have that connection needed because a contemporary lifestyle will not go far in this life or the next. Jeremiah 17:9 (NKJV) says,

"The heart is deceitful above all things, and desperately wicked" (Jeremiah 17:9 NKJV).

The difference between living a contemporary life and spiritual life is that contemporary life can easily bear false fruits. In contrast, spiritual practices help mature us as followers of Christ because of the Spirit's atoning work through salvation and enable the launch and perfecting of the kingdom of Heaven. Without the Spirit's work in us, our actions are ultimately influenced by the ruler of this world, which is Satan (2 Corinthians 4:4). It is crucial that we walk in the Spirit and have that deeper relationship with God through prayer and bring every thought captive to the obedience of Christ so that we can walk in the love he has called us to.

GOD'S COVENANTS WITH HUMANITY

A COVENANT IS AN AGREEMENT BETWEEN TWO or more individuals or groups that establishes their relationship with each other. Understanding of covenant is essential to understand the scriptures and God's interaction with humankind, the nation of Israel, and the Church. Throughout the scriptures, there are at least five different covenants that God created with certain people during the canonical history. Each covenantal relationship that was created set up for the next one to be established and fulfilled. The covenants that are extensively emphasized throughout scripture are the Adamic, Noahic, Abrahamic, Mosaic, Davidic, and New Covenant. In each of these covenants, God initiates, establishes, and fulfills the covenants either with a person, a group of people, or the whole world conditionally or unconditionally.

THE ADAMIC COVENANT

In the Adamic Covenant, there is part 1, before sin and death, and part 2, after sin and death entered the world. In the first part of it, God gave the task to have dominion and consecrate the earth.

"Then God said, Let Us make man in Our image, according to Our likeness; let them have dominion over the fish of the sea, over the birds of the air, and over the cattle, over all the earth and over every creeping thing that creeps on the earth. So, God created man in His own image; in the image of God He created him; male and female He created them." (Genesis 1:26-27 NKJV)

Through our dominion, man was given the task to replenish the earth. According to the Hebrew transliteration, the word "replenish" has a synonym which is "consecrate." Consecrate means to make or declare sacred; set apart or dedicate to the service of a deity.

"Therefore, since we are receiving a kingdom which cannot be shaken, let us have grace, by which we may serve God acceptably with reverence and godly fear. For our God is a consuming fire." Hebrews 12:28-29 (NKJV) God being a holy celestial creator, cannot walk anywhere without His holy fire cleansing the places He walks through. So, God gave the job to man for the earth to be a holy place so that He could dwell and fellowship with His creation. Part 1 of the covenant was created for fellowship. Because of man's sin and betrayal towards God, God himself initiated another covenant with man and made the redemption plan go into effect.

THE NOAHIC COVENANT

The response that God made to seeing humanity fall from grace was to create a newer covenant. In the Noahic covenant, God initiates His covenant with Noah and his family with promises of blessings. He reaffirms man's role on the earth and instructs how to treat every living creature. Along with His command that He initially gave to Adam and Eve, Noah was given additional instructions, including the consequences of one's actions, whether they are good or bad (Genesis 9:1-17). God reveals that He still chooses to reaffirm His command originally given to Adam and Eve, with the addition to the consequences of one's actions, whether they are good or bad. Even though He knows that the imagination of the heart of man is evil, He refuses to place another curse on all creation and commands the earth to flourish and do what it is made to do (Genesis 8:22).

God set up certain laws as part of the moral and ethical value system embedded in His nature.

"' So God blessed Noah and his sons, and said to them: 'Be fruitful and multiply, and fill the earth. And the fear of you and the dread of you shall be on every beast of the earth, on every bird of the air, on all that move *on* the earth, and on all the fish of the sea. They are given into your hand. Every moving thing that lives shall be food for you. I have given you all things, even as the green herbs. But you shall not eat flesh with its life, *that is,* its blood. Surely for your lifeblood I will demand *a reckoning;* from the hand of every beast I will require it, and from the hand of man. From the hand of every man's brother I will require the life of man'" (Genesis 9:1-5 NKJV).

In this covenant, God provided an unconditional covenant to Noah through a rainbow sign that He will never destroy humankind again. And a sign was given as a show of His promise of the covenant, a rainbow in a cloud. God fulfilled His part of the covenant by keeping the promises He made to Noah and the rest of humanity by not destroying the earth again with a flood despite the extensiveness of wickedness seen in the world.

THE ABRAHAMIC COVENANT

As we get to the Abrahamic Covenant, we see that God's direction is becoming narrower than the previous. Before this covenant, God was speaking directly to one person and his lineage. According to Genesis 12:1-9, God reveals to Abraham that God initiated it by promising Abraham that He would bless all of creation through his descendants.

"And I will make of you a great nation, and I will bless you and make your name great, so that you will be a blessing" (Genesis 12:2 NKJV)

It is seen that God established this covenant by making a promise to Abraham. According to it, Abraham will be made a great nation, he will be blessed, be a blessing, protected by God blessing and cursing others according to how they would treat him, and through him, all the families of the earth will be blessed.

The covenant was first introduced when God came to him in a dream and made certain promises to him as evidence of the covenant he wants to make. Genesis 16:13-21 gives evidence to the fact that God inaugurated the covenantal process through the sacrificing of an animal and circumcision of all the males under Abraham so that the fulfillment of the promises made would come to pass.

As a sign of the covenant, God blessed Abraham with the son he was promised. God affirmed an unalterable purpose in the unconditional promises given to

Abraham of Israel's continuation as a nation and possession of the promised land so that God can do His work in redeeming mankind. According to the covenant, Abraham will be made a great nation, he will be blessed, be a blessing, protected by God blessing and cursing others according to how they would treat him, and through him, all the families of the earth will be blessed.

Not only was Abraham given the son of promise, which was Isaac, he was also blessed with several other children who built nations of their own. Currently, we only know of seven of his children, as the children of his concubines were not mentioned, nor the concubines themselves (Genesis 25:1-6)

THE MOSAIC COVENANT

The creation of the Mosaic Covenant started off by God at Mount Sinai. It extended throughout the forty years in the wilderness, in which laws were given to the Israelites to follow to fulfill their purpose in being the light to the nations. What makes this covenant different from all the others is that it is classified as a Suzerain-Vassal type covenant where the authority figure is God Himself. It is a direct result and reaffirmation of

52

Abraham's covenant, which has come to pass along with Israel becoming a great nation.

The extent of the covenant made is seen in Exodus 20-31, in which through the covenant, laws were set in place. This covenant is conditional because it was considered only to be for a certain period. It was to continue until the coming of the promised seed, and the blessings and cursing were also given, as the outcome of when they obeyed or disobeyed them. It was made so that the people of Israel could mirror God's glory and holiness through the fulfillment of the Abrahamic promise.

The fulfillment of this covenant is seen as blessings were showered upon them when they were obedient to the law and cursing when they were disobedient. This covenant was created for the people directly under the Abrahamic covenant to live a life reflecting the God they serve, a holy and gracious God. They were given a chance to be able to speak to God just as Moses did with God, but His presence was too intense for them because all they knew were how to follow religious and ritualistic laws being enslaved by a foreign people for 400 years.

'Now when all the people saw the thunder and the flashes of lightning and the sound of the trumpet and the mountain smoking, the people were afraid and trembled, and they stood far off and said to Moses, "You speak to us, and we will listen; but do not let God speak to us, lest we die." Moses said to the people, "Do not fear, for God has come to test you, that the fear of him may be before you, that you may not sin." The people stood far off, while Moses drew near to the thick darkness where God was' (Exodus 20:18-21 ESV).

They refused the first-ever chance as a people to hear God personally and intimately the way their forefathers heard from and walked with God. Instead, they simply accepted the laws without a personal relationship. Without it, following the laws would result in judgments regarding their actions. With the law and relationship together, the law would be in their hearts, and the Holy Spirit would be moving them to walk according to the right path.

THE DAVIDIC COVENANT

The Davidic covenant includes the promise of a seed, a kingdom, a great name, a place for the people, rest from his enemies, and a house for the God of all creation. It is a continuation of God's covenant with Israel, yet more specified. In which David's lineage was going to bless all of creation through God's reign on earth. And they brought in the ark of the LORD and set it in its place, inside the tent that David had pitched for it. And David offered burnt offerings and peace offerings before the LORD (2 Samuel 6:17 ESV).

David created a tabernacle as part of the sign of the covenantal relationship between him and God, which goes in deeper than how things worked in the Old Testament.

'Now when the king lived in his house and the Lord had given him rest from all his surrounding enemies, the king said to Nathan the prophet,

"See now, I dwell in a house of cedar, but the ark of God dwells in a tent'" (2 Samuel 7:1-2 ESV). Also, God initiates His covenant with David when he thinks of making a house for God when He Himself is residing in a magnificent palace. The difference between this and all other covenants is that this one had conditional and unconditional parts. The unconditional promise was that the house of David will always reign over Israel, his name would be made great, and God would bless all the nations ultimately through his seed (2 Samuel 7:12). Through this promise, the messiah would come through his lineage as an establishment of God's intimate relationship with David.

"And the government shall be upon His shoulder, and His name shall be called, Wonderful Counselor, Mighty God, Everlasting Father, Prince of Peace. Of the increase of His government and of peace there will be no end, on the throne of David and over His kingdom, to establish it and to uphold it with justice and with righteousness from this time forth and forevermore" (Isaiah 9:6-7 ESV). The promise of rest and a place for the people were conditional promises, in which their hearts had to be in the right place and following God for it to be fulfilled in their lives. As seen by the evidence revealed, this Davidic covenant narrows further down to David's lineage, and through him, the nations of the earth would be blessed.

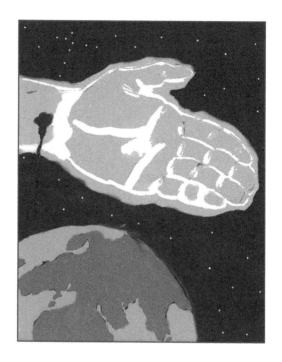

THE NEW COVENANT

The New Covenant is the final contract between God and man in the canonical text, which all other covenants were created to lead up to (Galatians 3:15-22).

"Now the promises were made to Abraham and to his offspring. It does not say, "And to offsprings," referring to many, but referring to one, "And to your offspring," who is Christ. This is what I mean: the law, which came 430 years afterward, does not annul a covenant previously ratified by God, to make the promise void. For if the inheritance comes by the law, it no longer comes by promise; but God gave it to Abraham by a promise. Why then the law? It was added because of transgressions, until the offspring should come to whom the promise had been made, and it was put in place through angels by an intermediary. Now an intermediary implies more than one, but God is one. Is the law then contrary to the promises of God? Certainly not! For if a law had been given that could give life, then righteousness would indeed be by the law. But the Scripture imprisoned everything under sin, so that the promise by faith in Jesus Christ might be given to those who believe." (Galatians 3:15-22). The difference between this and all the other covenants is that it is categorized as a blood covenant. The new covenant's impact is seen through the covenantal breaking of bread during Passover, in which the covenant of blood is magnified.

The initiation of the covenant started as soon as man sinned (Genesis 3:15). It shows us how much God cares about us and how much he wants us to be rescued from our bondage of sin and death. He wanted to fulfill the promise He made to Adam, and He finally gets to come through with it in this new covenant.

"For God so loved the world, that he gave his only Son, that whoever believes in Him should not perish but have eternal life" (John 3:16 ESV).

The establishment of the covenant was done through the death and resurrection of Jesus on the cross of Calvary with the promise of eternal life in heaven for those who believe in Him as Lord.

Along with the establishment of the Church and the promise of the Holy Spirit, the third Godhead of the Trinity is an unconditional promise to the world.

"Behold, the days are coming, declares the Lord, when I will make a new covenant with the house of Israel and the house of Judah, not like the covenant that I made with their fathers on the day when I took them by the hand to bring them out of the land of Egypt, my covenant that they broke, though I was their husband, declares the Lord. For this is the covenant that I will make with the house of Israel after those days, declares the Lord: I will put my law within them, and I will write it on their hearts. And I will be their God, and they shall be my people. And no longer shall each one teach his neighbor and each his brother, saying, 'Know the Lord,' for they shall all know me, from the least of them to the greatest, declares the Lord. For I will forgive their iniquity, and I will remember their sin no more." (Jeremiah 31:31-34 ESV)

A covenant is a promise of a specific type of agreement between two or more parties to establish a relationship, which benefits all parties. The biblical concept of covenant involves God's promises to certain individuals, people, and the world. God reveals through the scriptures the essential covenants He initiated with certain figures to redeem humankind. These were the Noahic, Abrahamic, Mosaic, Davidic, and new covenants.

Each covenant was a greater emphasis and fulfillment of the prior ones committed. As each is made, the next becomes even more detailed than the previous in the commitment of all of creation being saved through the Abrahamic lineage. Jeremiah 31:31-34 gives us the knowledge of God vowing an upcoming point in time when He will renew His covenant with the Church so that His own covenantal authenticity brings His people to a full realization of redemption through Him. Therefore, the purpose of initiating, establishing, and fulfilling these covenants, God intended to establish a relationship with mankind and ultimately their redemption.

OUR MANDATE
AS BELIEVERS

THE GREAT COMMISSION GIVEN BY JESUS instructs to "Go therefore and make disciples of all nations, baptizing them in the name of the Father, and of the Son, and of the Holy Spirit" (Matthew 28:18-20). Jesus also told His disciples to wait in Jerusalem for the Father's promise, which is Holy Spirit, who will give gifts to exercise their God-given mission dynamically. These gifts given through baptism and discipleship gave the ability for the body of Christ to perform different functions and ultimately be used to reach and edify different groups of people. Through these divine gifts, the Church was not only able to just spread the Gospel to all of creation but to bless them as they go, just as Jesus said in Luke 6.

The dictionary definition of a disciple is one who is a pupil or advocate of the doctrines of another. 1 John 4:8 says, "He who does not love does not know God, for God is love." A disciple is someone who overcomes the trials and worldly pleasures that this life has to offer and becomes more like Jesus, and this process requires a response to the Holy Spirit's prompting to examine the heart of oneself.

"Give, and it will be given to you: good measure, pressed down, shaken together, and running over will be put into your bosom. For with the same measure that you use, it will be measured back to you." (Luke 6:38)

God, Himself is the definition of what love is. Through His love, He has given so much of Himself to His creation. Because He is a giving God, He cannot hold this *AGAPE* to Himself. Agape is a selfless and never-ending form of love. He created us for Himself. He created us in His image and likeness. He had to create something that resembles Him, something that was capable of receiving His love.

Therefore, it is human nature to have a sense of belonging. I would go as far as even saying that it is in

God's nature to have a sense of belonging, which is why we were created. Also, we may also give those around us a part of who and what we are. Because He is a God of Love, when we choose to love others despite the circumstances, we are opening the door of their lives so that God Himself can pour it out onto their lives as well. That way, they can have that God encounter that would rebirth their spirit into the fullness of all that He is.

Our hope as believers is looking forward to spending our eternal life with the God who created and redeemed us. The eschatological time frame of Jesus coming had been written in the skies since the dawn of time. Understanding this eschatology of the nature of the Christian hope that is based on Jesus's establishment of His kingdom is the hope that we look forward to as Christians. God's kingdom was a mystery that was hidden to the Old Testament saints. John the Baptist came to prepare the kingdom of God.

"In those days, John the Baptist came preaching in the wilderness, and saying, 'Repent for the kingdom of Heaven is at hand'" (Matthew 3:2 NKJV).

According to the scriptures, John was the first to introduce the coming of the kingdom of Heaven. Later, through Jesus' ministry, He explained His kingdom's workings with evidence of it through signs and wonders that followed Him wherever He went. Through the scriptures, Christian eschatology reveals how the kingdom of Heaven is present and yet not fully consummated and how the final restoration of it shapes the present kingdom work of believers today.

Jesus introduces the Gospel of the kingdom as he spreads this message across the land of Israel. Jesus goes around declaring that the countdown has finally hit zero and that the promises of the ages have finally come into fruition. The evidence of the kingdom of Heaven being present is through the evidence of the manifestations of the signs and wonders that followed Jesus wherever He went. Signs and wonders were even following His followers as well. Through His gospel message, which no one has ever done before through the cleansing of the leper, healing of the sick, and raising the dead. Even though the kingdom of God is already present, there must be an invitation to get in. Just as it takes a Visa of some sort to enter a country, there must be an invitation received and accepted. Jesus handed us an invitation through the cross, but it isn't fully realized that not many have accepted this invitation into the kingdom that God has prepared for his creation.

"Assuredly, I say to you, whoever does not receive the kingdom of God as a little child will by no means enter it" (Mark 10:15 NKJV)

When heaven and earth are finally going to be in sync with one another, our bodies will be transformed to the likeness of Christ. When Jesus returned to Heaven, He didn't just take back His old appearance but kept His image and resemblance as He was on earth. He kept His wounds in His arms, side, and feet as a reminder to all creation that mankind belongs to Him and Him alone. In his letter, Peter says that God brings about the last days, which is a sort of resistance to Caesar's new empirical power as He chose to conform time to His own bidding. Romans 8:29 articulates that we who have been chosen will be transformed to the image of Christ. Matthew 16:19 says that He has given us the keys to his kingdom, and whatever we bind or loose on earth will be bound or loosed in heaven as well. With these keys, he has given the Church, His body, the same power that raised Him from the dead to do the work of the ministry and revealing His kingdom on the earth.

The emphasis of the kingdom of Heaven was only glimpsed at from a distance from the time sin and death entered the world. The appearance of Jesus Christ on the earth was anticipated since the beginning of the earth's foundation and is the core of the age-old Jewish prophecies that humanity had been waiting for. As a follower of Jesus Christ, the eschatology regarding the hope of the Christian faith is significant in that it is what every believer looks forward to. The hope of receiving a reward is not the grounds and incentive of the eschatology revealed by Jesus, it is about incorporating the will that God has and the demonstrations of Jesus into how we ought to walk in our daily lives.

"Now it shall come to pass in the latter days That the mountain of the Lord's house Shall be established on the top of the mountains, and shall be exalted above the hills; And all nations shall flow to it" (Isaiah 2:2 NKJV).

The eschatology of the Gospel divulges how the kingdom of Heaven is present and yet not fully completed and the way the final restoration of it as it influences the way we walk in our daily lives. This was the ultimate hidden mystery of the ages that was hidden in the heart of God, which was finally revealed through the life of Christ. This power that was revealed through the death and resurrection was given to the Church to live and act in the same manner, which is through the Holy Spirit of God.

Walking in love without any partiality is an essential factor of living a Christian life. When Moses was given the law for the people, each law can be categorized under one primary umbrella: love the Lord your God with all your heart, soul, and mind. In having a relationship with the Creator above, the love of God will begin to reveal itself. As God's love is being uncovered, your identity in Him will be shown and will cause you to love yourself on a much deeper level. As that love is being realized, the love for the neighbor will also flow out. Throughout the scriptures, it is seen that one of the royal laws given by God is to love your neighbor as yourself

(James 2:8). In Philippians 4, Paul says to "Greet every saint in Christ Jesus. The brethren who are with me greet you. All the saints greet you, but especially those who are of Caesar's household. The grace of our Lord Jesus Christ be with you all. Amen" (NKJV).

Today, the revelation of this passage of scripture can still be applied in each person's day-to-day lives. As Paul brings to light the royal law of loving your neighbor, he goes in-depth in 1 Corinthians 3. He states that when you stand before the throne room of God, everything you have ever done will be set on fire, and you will receive your reward according to what remains. In 1 Corinthians 13, it says that if we spoke with tongues of angels, gave our bodies to the fire, gave prophetic words, or understood all the mysteries of the world, but didn't have love, it wouldn't profit us a thing. Hebrews 12:29 states that God is a holy consuming fire, and 1 John 4:8 shares that God is love in all his essence.

With this knowledge, when you stand before the throne room of God, everything that you have ever done out of the love of God is what will only remain when everything is set on fire. With all the racial segregation going on today, it is crucial to keep this passage in mind. We ought to love one another as we are all part of the body of Christ regardless of our cultural background or skin color.

"But he who is joined to the Lord is one spirit with Him" (1 Corinthians 6:17 NKJV).

Jesus has called us to do greater works than what He did on this earth. Wherever you are at in life, that's where your ministry is for that moment. Jesus' life was His ministry. He calls us -His Bride- to do greater works than what He did.

The Creator wants His creation to do greater works than what He did. The prototype is God, and we are the archetype. Every part of us is the exact replica of God Almighty.

And He calls us to do greater things than what He did while He was on this earth.

He sat with sinners and transformed their lives.

We ought to eat with a multitude of sinners and change their lives with the love of God that was poured out on us. Jesus spoke, and the demons fled. We stand our ground and don't even must speak, and they flee.

Jesus' garment brought healing and power into the lives that touched it. Our presence in a town will bring revival because of the power given to us and Holy Spirit.

We Have No Limits.

"I can do all things through Christ who strengthens me." (Philippians 4:13)

It is time to step out in faith.

If you feel led by Holy Spirit to do something radical, Do It, even if no one follows you.

The power of God will fall on you because you stepped out in faith to do something radical, and you will reap a massive harvest of souls for the Kingdom.

So I say be radical and put no limits of boundaries before you where you may cap the power of God in your life. He emanates His power through His all-encompassing love that constantly flows out of Him. This is what we were made for. This spoken word that I wrote many years ago tells us a portion of God's love story to us.

We were made in the image of Love
We were made to Love and be loved by Him
We were made for intimacy

We were made to experience the relentless, burning, fiery, unreasonable,

unimaginable Love of the Father

We were made to be forever in His arms,

forever in His presence

When we lose sight of that we look to other means to feel love,

either with people, or by drowning out the hole with a

feeling of pleasure

Understanding the Love of God is where our focus should be

The Lord has called us to love

We need to know His love more deeply, and THAT Love

passes all understanding

The world shall know us by our Love for one another

Behold what manner of Love the Father has bestowed upon

us that we should be called children of God

He gave His greatest treasure, His greatest Love, the desire

of His heart, that we might know His love, that we might

know His burning passionate and amazing Love

He says, "you are My Love, you are My life, you are My

bride, you are My joy, you are My portion, you are by

beloved, you are My child.

I have given you everything, what else do you want? I made it all for you, it is My gift to you.

There is nothing more that you need to do.

Rest in My love for you.

Trust Me, believe Me, but above all Love Me.

Hear My voice, My darling, My child.

Follow close, don't turn your head away, look to Me.

Let's rule the world together!"

The Lord created the universe by speaking and we were made in His image and according to His likeness, so when we speak what should happen?

The God of the universe, the Most High God who speaks world into existence is in love with you!

Proverbs 18:21 says, "Death and life are in the power of the tongue, and those who love it will eat its fruit."

Why are our words so powerful? According to scientific research, it shows us that it is impossible to speak without breathing. Genesis 2:7 says, "And the Lord God formed man of the dust of the ground, and breathed into his nostrils the breath of life; and man became a living being." When God breathed into man,

He planted His divine power to make us alive. That is why for in Him we live and move and have our being (Acts 17:28).

Science has proven to us that through this God-given breath that we breathe, that hits our vocal cords to create the voice that we each have. Even more scientific research has shown us in many different instances, when you speak life over plants, they blossom, but when you speak ill over them, they wither away. Therefore, our words are so powerful. Matthew 12:36 tells us, "But I tell you that everyone will have to give account on the day of judgment for every empty word they have spoken."

In Matthew 25:12-30, Jesus shares the *Parable of the Talents*, where the master had given each of his servants a certain amount of "talents." In this parable, talents are a form of currency used in that time frame. But God showed me something unique from that. Each of us has been given a specific talent and ability that our Master had invested in us. Whatever gifts and skills that we each have as individuals are meant for something more. It was not meant to be kept away as the last servant did in the parable.

We must speak the realm of Heaven into existence on this earth through the gifts and talents given to us so that we may bless His creation. There is a need for this generation. God is trying to talk to you so that you may fulfill His glory through you. We must step out in faith and use what was given to fulfill the path our Father in Heaven has laid out for us. Every day we walk by homeless people, ignore drug addicts, make fun of the outcast, damn the party-goers, the abandoned, abused, fatherless, prostitutes, gangsters, widows, and even homosexuals. Whenever we walk by them or damn them, we don't realize that these are the people Jesus came to save!

A couple of years ago, a few of my friends and I decided to do something radical. To give a little bit of an understanding of how we were able to, let's look at how Paul reached out to the Greek community to minister the Gospel. In Acts 17, we see that Paul noticed the Greeks worshipping a statue that had no name and no one knew which God that was, but out of respect, they prayed and offered sacrifices to it. Through the meekness of wisdom (James 3:13), Paul found a way of connecting and relating with the community by gaining an understanding of this idol they were worshipping and was able to communicate the Gospel through that connection. Meekness is strength under control. For example, when playing with a baby, you do not use all your strength. Otherwise, you will fatally harm the baby. Instead, you play according to the strength of the baby. In the same way, we must use wisdom, which Paul used to connect and communicate with the Greek community.

We decided to go to such an unconventional place to bring the Gospel, which was a rave! We took the same aspect of what Paul did and found a way of connecting with the rave community. We found out that they follow something called PLUR Peace, Love, Unity, and Respect. At a rave, when you "vibe" or have that connection with someone, you PLUR with them and do a type of handshake. First, you each do the peace sign, the heart sign, then interlock fingers with each other and exchange candy bracelets. So, three days before the rave, we spent time in prayer and fasting. We were asking the Lord for encouraging words, words of knowledge, prophetic words, and such. As you can see in this picture, we created quite a bit of them.

By the end of the night, we had given all of them away, and every single person we came across was receptive to the Gospel as we were able to communicate through their understanding and loved on them. We connected several of them to different churches in the area, and we even bumped into a couple of other ministry teams while we were there. God really moved as we brought the light of God into such a dark place, and lives were transformed that day.

All this happens because of the relationship built with God as a family member and being a friend of God. "And the Scripture was fulfilled which says, "Abraham believed God, and it was accounted to him for righteousness." And he was called the friend of God" (James 2:23) because of the relationship that Abraham built with our Creator, God Himself called Abraham, His friend. And so, when you are in a friendship with God, you are going into a deeper relationship with Holy Spirit, and you are not focusing on the ministry, but the core of it, which is a relationship with Him. Because you choose to focus on the relationship with Him, you can go into deeper realms and increase your capacity to do more. But, when you decide to focus more on your ministry that God called you into, you become more task-oriented. You become more of a servant rather than a friend.

When you focus with a servant mindset, your focus caps Holy Spirit's ability to the limit of your ministry or title. Bill Johnson, the Senior Pastor of Bethel Church in Redding, California, gave this great scenario, "When you have this famous friend who chooses to come to visit your house often and then you tell your friends and neighbors about the time and place of when they would arrive. After some time, your famous friend will notice that you are only using them for the resources that they must do "the work" rather than spend quality time and relationship with Him. When He sees this, He will stop coming and you are left with what had already been given and nothing more."

In the same way, when we choose to focus on the ministry or title, although God-given, more than your relationship with the One who gave it to you, you are diminishing His ability to work in your life. The difference between a servant and a friend is that a servant only knows the to-do list given to them. But a friend knows the deeper things of God and the reasoning for what is being done and about to be done. "No longer do I call you servants, for a servant does not know what his master is doing; but I have called you friends, for all things that I heard from My Father I have made known to you" (John 15:15). "The secret of the Lord is with those who fear Him, And He will show them His covenant" (Psalm 25:14).

As children and friends of the Most High God, we need to change our perspective. We must step out of our comfort zone to prove to the lost the real meaning of being a Christian. Jesus gave us the command to preach to the whole world that He is the only way to salvation. He didn't ask us. He COMMANDED us. What are you waiting for? Remember, He created us in HIS image!!! We have ALL His attributes, and we can see that in our society, our culture, our family life, and everywhere in our day-to-day lives. His Love is so deep that it is unfathomable. Man, He loves us so much that He was risking being sent to Hell for eternity just so that YOU can be in Heaven!

The root of all ministry is the love of God, to love Him and to be loved by Him. 1 Corinthians 13 gives us such clear evidence of that. No matter how many souls we save, no matter how "spirit-filled" we might be, even if we become martyrs, if it is not done through the love of God, it is all meaningless. It's the love of God that changes us. It is only through the love of God that anything can indeed happen. It is the core of the law that was given to Moses on Mount Sinai. Jesus summed up all the commandments into two. "'You shall love the Lord your God with all your heart, with all your soul, and with all your mind.' This is the first and great commandment. And the second is like it: 'You shall love your neighbor as yourself'" (Matthew 22:37-39).

Through friendship and relationship with Him, we are able to scratch the surface of understanding His love for us. From that, we can love Him back and love ourselves for the way that He loves us. When we are finally able to see this, we begin to have the capacity to love our neighbor as ourselves.

Just as the roots of a tree give off nutrients for the branches, which in turn feed the surrounding air with oxygen. The leaves from the branches bring in the air's carbon dioxide and go deep into the roots to feed the soil. Where you are grounded and surrounded by impacts the community you are part of. But you get to choose if the surroundings influence and affect you or will you be the one to influence and affect your surroundings?

Knowing that, how much more wouldn't you want to reach out to all those lost souls around us? Come, let us arise, for, through Christ, we are the light amid the darkness. Where there is light, darkness will NEVER prevail.

All this to show how important it is to know the Father, Son, and Holy Spirit through intimacy as three persons, yet One God. How all three are intricately woven into our lives from the very construct of time. How every aspect of human existence represents the union of the Trinity. Despite man being deceived and falling into sin, the plan for redemption was set in motion so that the gap can be bridged once again so that we may coexist and fellowship with the One that created us. The glory of man has always been to fully reveal the glory of God in and through our lives. "We can all draw close to him with the veil removed from our faces. And with no veil we all become like mirrors who brightly reflect the glory of the Lord Jesus.

We are being transfigured into His very image as we move from one brighter level of glory to another. And this glorious transfiguration comes from the Lord, who is the Spirit." (2 Corinthians 3:18 TPT).

Our mandate has always been to make every place we step to be a holy place, so that God Himself can dwell with us. To not only live a life in a manner that pleases the Lord, but one that blesses everyone and everything around us. The only way that we can overcome the principalities and powers of darkness, is through God's love flowing in and through us daily.

Jesus' lifestyle reveals the two greatest commandments, which the commandments of the law summarize into. "So he answered and said, "You shall love the Lord your God with all your heart, with all your soul, with all your strength, and with all your mind,' and 'your neighbor as yourself'" (Luke 10:27). "For if there is first a willing mind, it is accepted according to what one has, and not according to what he does not have" (2 Corinthians 8:12). We can't give to others what we do not have. As we begin to understand the love of God for ourselves, we begin to not only love God back, but also love ourselves as well. As we start to love ourselves the way that God loves us, then only can we love our neighbors AND enemies the way that God loves YOU.

REFERENCES:

Blue Letter Bible application.

Compilation of several of my essays put together from my time at Grand Canyon University. 2017-2020.

Direct quote from Dr. Luke Hoselton. Christian Worldview Professor at Grand Canyon University.

Lucado, Max. Grace for The Moment.

Selah. *How Deep the Father's Love for Us*. Album: You Deliver Me. 2009.

The Holy Bible.

The Nicene Creed. The First Council of Nicaea. 325 AD.

CPSIA information can be obtained
at www.ICGtesting.com
Printed in the USA
BVHW090008190521
607645BV00008B/1258

9 781662 816062